From Poles to Pews:

How America's Most Infamous Strip Club Became a Church

Dan M. Garrett

From Poles to Pews
Dan M. Garrett

Copyright © 2024 by Dan M.

Garrett All rights reserved.

Table of Contents

Dedication

"I can't wait!" was Becca McClendon's exclamation when I told her about my plans to start a church in Buckhead. I was equally excited because I had known this awesome young lady since she was a child, and I knew she would add her limitless enthusiasm to our new church family as well as bring a bunch of friends with her.

In the 1980s, as youth minister of a church with about 2,000 members, I was involved in many significant life situations of young people and their families, but none quite like Becca.

At the age of eight, Becca was diagnosed with childhood cancer. At her mother's encouragement, I was invited into their journey. I would go with Becca to doctor visits, hold her hand during painful treatments, sit in the waiting room for hours telling stories trying to lighten the mood, and, almost always, having prayer with her and her stressed family.

Becca made it through leukemia a stronger and more faith-filled person. She graduated from high school, went to college, and got a job in the city. In an unfortunate turn, as an adult, she was diagnosed with cancer again, and after a lengthy ordeal, passed into the presence of the Lord, January 2007.

I dedicate this book to Becca in memory of her courage, tenacity, faith, laughter, and the many lessons she taught a million friends about loyalty and love. She truly lived out the mission of the church to welcome and show love to every person.

Becca, we miss you. We know we will all be reunited one day. I can't wait!

INTRODUCTION

Rest in Peace

Sometimes I think about what my obituary will say. I also wonder how a synopsis can fully capture one's entire life in three paragraphs, along with a quick headline focusing on the person's most outstanding and memorable trait. Through the years, I have spoken professionally to over two million people, created a seminar attended by 10,000 parents and teens, and raised a ton of money for various causes. But ... I am confident the headline for my obituary will read: *Strip Club Preacher Passes!*

Honestly, I'm okay with that, because turning the Gold Club into God's Club was one of the greatest things I've ever experienced. Starting a church in a dilapidated old building where men used to pay lots of money to look at barely-clothed women was the most challenging, energizing, strangest, riskiest, and thrilling thing I have ever done!

I share this story with you because it is a beautiful metaphor of how God works in our lives. It is also an encouraging saga of people working together, especially as we discovered our shared humanity.

We learned so much about ourselves and others during the process of cleaning out a cruddy facility and turning it into a place of gathering and worship. We learned about not judging those different from us. We learned humility, depending on each other and what it means to lean on a higher power. This job looked way too big for us, and it was … only God's divine guidance could accomplish such a daunting task in a short time.

As we journey through the God's Club story together, I hope you, too, will see how God's hand was at work, and may it touch your spirit and inspire you to take risks and step out in faith.

CHAPTER ONE:

The Most Famous Strip Club in America

C andy's presence commanded the stage. As one of the Gold Club's most popular dancers, the crowd really responded to her "act." The bass thumped hard and loud in the speakers. The patrons, mostly male, probably could not name the song, but they were not there for a concert. Instead, they were there to watch Candy and others dance ... and take off their clothes.

Many of these guys dropped $300 a night. Some spent $2,000 entertaining business clients. It was easy to do. When you first entered, you just gave the man at the door your credit card. He would scan it and give you Gold Bucks (like monopoly money) to spend on drinks and lap dances. Twenty-two years old, Candy was addicted to methamphetamine and had a sexually transmitted disease. But the crowd really liked her act.

Candy was proud to work at the Gold Club, one of Atlanta's premier "gentlemen's venues." Many local business people report that the first request commonly made by out-of-town clients visiting Atlanta on business trips was, "Take me to the Gold Club.

The club admitted over one million patrons in five-plus years.

Frequented by all types of celebrities, limousines would pull under the gold awning and out would step renowned sports stars, actors, and politicians. They stepped into a modest building, checked in at the front counter, and walked into a darkened two-story open space, with brightly colored lights flashing and neon light strips lining the wall. The main level featured a stage surrounded by tall tables and stools. Overstuffed leather chairs and small tables for drinks interspersed the room. Within close access were a cigar stand and two bars. Higher paying patrons sat in the surrounding balcony, looking down on the activities below. Private rooms were upstairs and rented for exclusive parties and private lap dances, along with plenty more illegal and immoral activities.

Periodically, the club would be in the news for alleged mafia connections, suspicious activity, and occasional sex scandals. Eventually it was raided by federal agents and closed, making national headlines.

In November 1999, Gold Club owner Steve Kaplan and other club employees, including dancers, were indicted on a full array of federal racketeering charges, including credit card fraud, prostitution, money laundering, police corruption, and even inappropriate ties to the powerful Gambino crime family.

Former Gold Club manager Thomas Sicignano — nicknamed Ziggy — charged that Kaplan over several years "orchestrated" a series of sexual events involving professional athletes and other favored customers, including athletes in the NBA, MLB, NFL, wrestling, and stars in the movie and music industries. No athlete was convicted of committing a crime.

Midway through a sensational trial in August 2001, Kaplan brokered a plea bargain with federal prosecutors. He pleaded guilty to racketeering and was sentenced to sixteen months in federal prison and ordered to pay a $5 million forfeiture and $250,000 in restitution. Most of the other defendants also entered into plea agreements for reduced sentences.

The FBI padlocked the doors and the Gold Club closed … for good.

CHAPTER TWO:

Into the Unknown

I moved to Atlanta, Georgia, following my time in college and seminary in Cincinnati, Ohio, when I was twenty-four years old. With its rich history, Atlanta is home to a large number of international company headquarters (most notably, Coca-Cola, Home Depot, and UPS) and has a terrific mix of people from a variety of backgrounds.

Atlanta birthed the civil rights movement, and serves as home to the Martin Luther King, Jr. Center for Nonviolent Social Change. Thousands of lives are shaped at influential colleges and graduate schools, including Emory University, Georgia Institute of Technology, Georgia State University, Columbia Seminary, and Morehouse College.

The city was home for many years to sizable churches of influence, but the 1970s and 80s saw diminished church attendance as members began moving to the suburbs. Some churches chose to follow the crowd outside the city limits. A few large churches remained, but there seemed to be a void, especially with regards to communicating with the growing demographic of those in their twenties and thirties.

At the southern end of the city sits State Farm Arena and the World Congress Center. As Peachtree Street winds its way northward, the middle section of Atlanta is known as Midtown, featuring the historic Fox Theatre (where the movie *Gone With the Wind* premiered), Georgia Tech, and the city's original Krispy Kreme donut shop. (I only mention Krispy Kreme because this is supposed to be a spiritual book, and interacting with a cream-filled, chocolate-frosted donut is a spiritual experience for me!) The northern section of town is identified as Buckhead. This is the cultural center, the premier shopping destination, and home to many major hotels, as well as 95,000 residents who dwell in neighborhoods, condominiums, and apartments.

Buckhead is home to upscale shopping centers like Lenox Square Mall and Phipps Plaza, which include Neiman Marcus and Saks Fifth Avenue stores. This area is famous for the number and variety of restaurants.

On the east side of Atlanta is the city of Decatur, where I ministered to youth at a large church. I was fortunate to work with these teens and families for eleven years during which I served as chaplain with the Southwest DeKalb High School football team and volunteered with Camp Sunshine for children with cancer.

Due to so many teenagers losing their lives to drinking and driving, I helped my friend Jack Mathis begin the Arrive Alive program which held assemblies in middle and high schools across the state, empowering young people to make positive choices. I spoke to approximately one million young people over the course of ten years.

One of the best parts of this time was meeting my wife Carol, getting married, and having our two children, a boy and a girl, Campbell and Danielle. Following eleven years of youth ministry, and while still traveling and speaking nationally, my family and I left Atlanta and moved ninety minutes south to pastor a church in Mayberry. Well, it wasn't actually Mayberry, the fictional idyllic town made famous in the *Andy Griffith Show*, but Lanett, Alabama, was very close. Downtown consisted of a dozen stores on the main street, with three traffic lights, surrounded by quiet neighborhoods with modest houses, and kids riding their bikes in the streets.

There was little crime, no traffic jams, and most everyone was friendly and generally happy. I pastored Spring Road Church for eight wonderful years. The church grew from fifty to over 300 members. The people in the church and the area embraced my wife and my two young children, and the ministry thrived although I began to yearn for a bigger challenge. I had no idea my prayer was about to be answered by having lunch in Atlanta.

In the spring of 2002, I met with some ministry friends at Perimeter Mall. I sat with Tim Stephens, a representative of a church funding organization, and someone I knew only as an acquaintance. During the conversation he suggested the need for a church in the heart of Atlanta. I tried to change the subject. I was sharp enough to know that God uses conversations like this to disrupt your life! But as Tim and I talked, something stirred within me as I considered the fact that there were so many people in Buckhead who surely needed the joy of knowing the Lord.

For the next few weeks, I couldn't shake the tug I felt. I began praying and sensing a need to initiate a spiritual outpost in this vital area of Georgia's capital city. Buckhead is the financial district for Atlanta and for the Southeast. It is truly the "Manhattan of the South," and I envisioned a new family of God coming alongside influential individuals as they navigated life's challenges. And, honestly, I contemplated the impact that Buckhead followers of Jesus could have in the world through their extensive business networks and significant financial capacity.

Wrestling with a "call" is a multilayered concept, filled with times of doubt, questioning, and fear. You pray, hoping to hear a voice from the skies. You write down your thoughts, making lists of pros and cons. You discuss with trusted friends, and of course, your spouse. Carol and I talked throughout this process. As an entrepreneur-type male, I saw all the possibilities. As a steady-as-she-goes type female, Carol was more aware of the practical implications, such as the impact on the kids, of leaving our small town, and the costs associated with heading back into the city.

In July, the annual gathering of Christian churches was held in Columbus, Ohio. A number of leaders in the church-planting movement circled up with me and Carol, and we brainstormed what a Buckhead project would look like. After more than two hours of dreaming and dialoguing, the group proposed that I was the man for the job. Carol and I could think of a number of reasons why this was not a preferable route for us, but agreed to think and pray about it.

On our family trip to the beach later in the summer, we had many discussions as a couple about Buckhead, but neither of us wanted to allow ourselves to get enthused about what we knew would be a giant disruption of our comfort zones. While I delayed seeking God's leading (in order not to deal with it!), Carol began praying, which initiated a tremendous season in her life of communicating with the Father, speaking her heart and deepest concerns to him, and then clearly hearing back from him.

Almost on a daily basis, Carol heard from the Lord through her weekly Community Bible Study, a speaker on the radio, a Sunday school lesson, or her own personal study. I would come home in the evening and she would say, "Well, guess what my devotional book was about today?" And then she would tell me it was something like: if you are going to follow God, you must be ready to let go of your comforts. Carol's enthusiastic reports sent strong signals of affirmation as I began to spend more time in prayer as well.

Similar to Carol's journey, I would hear a teaching on sacrifice and taking a risk. As we listened, read, and prayed, both of us received many confirmations such as these. Carol and I realized the road ahead of us included telling the kids, selling the house, moving, buying a house in pricey Atlanta, and much more stress. But we knew we had to go.

I had loved the city since I was twenty-four. And now my heart was beating for the very special and unique area of

Buckhead. The demographics indicated over 55 percent of people who live there were not affiliated with a church … a spiritual desert. I knew I must do this.

CHAPTER THREE:

"You're Doing What?"

R eactions from friends and family members to our decision to leave small town security and head into the challenging mission field of the big city fell into five categories:

1. Questioning my sanity.

2. Criticizing and doubting the project.

3. Laughing.

4. Focusing on the challenges involved.

5. Catching the vision and affirming.

Many asked, "Why would you leave such a good situation to go do something with so many unknowns?"

I always felt like I was getting mixed signals as the person's voice was saying, "Oh, that's great," while their face clearly exclaimed, "Are you crazy?" Some verbalized, or at least implied, "At your age, doing something this risky and leaving a good salary?" I served as pastor for eight years with a terrific group of people, many of whom were wealthy, so the perception was that I had a great setup.

At a conference, I spoke with the pastor of one of the largest churches in the nation at the time and informed him of my goal of planting in Buckhead. He said, "That's going to be tough."

This discouraged me a little as I was hoping for an affirmation or even some sort of blessing for my new venture.

At the same event, another minister said, "Glad it's you and not me." This was also disconcerting and hurt my feelings. But as I thought about the comment and reflected on his rather unremarkable ministry, I was glad it was me and not him, too, because I wanted this project to succeed!

A few other pastors said "good luck" in that tone of voice that suggested I would need a whole lot of it.

Buckhead is one of the wealthiest zip codes in America, so I was not surprised by some of the reactions locally. I heard comments like, "Buckhead people are so snobby," or "Everybody who lives there is so stuck-up."

Basically, these commentators revealed their prejudice against those in higher income brackets and all those who lived in this area of town. Their close-mindedness, either birthed in hatred toward the rich, or simply from being intimidated by those they don't understand, restricted them from having a ministry heart toward thousands of individuals and families who needed God's love.

Personal criticism usually comes in the side door as most people don't express their judgmental opinions straight to your face. I heard from friends that some ministers felt that "Dan just wants to be with the rich people." Some of this comes from the fact that I had served in two congregations which had a fair representation of families with money, so I had heard this sort of stereotyping before. The comments still stung, though, because I felt called by God to Buckhead. Plus, I was sacrificing a stable situation for the totally unknown. My family was uprooting from church, friends, and comfort, and I was stepping away from my national speaking opportunities to devote myself full time to this incredibly challenging task. All this hardly seemed worth it to just be able to "hang out with rich people."

And one other fact that many missed: everyone in Buckhead is not rich. While neighborhoods do mainly consist of families in the upper income brackets, there are a large number of young singles sharing an apartment with friends and married couples renting condominiums. The demographic of Buckhead includes a variety of incomes and backgrounds.

Besides, my philosophy has always been—wealthy people need to go to heaven, too. In addition to the fact that every person is a child of God, made in his image, and created for fellowship with him, everyone deserves to hear about the amazing grace that saves, renews, and restores us. Plus, a person with financial means can have such a positive effect and help ministry projects in so many ways. You would think pastors would get that. I always feel sorry for people who reveal their small-mindedness and pettiness as they stereotype those who are farther up the financial ladder.

Another type of reaction was focused on the many challenges of ministering in a diverse setting. Again, stereotypes came into play, but mixed with some realities as well. Many friends and supporters would comment that, "City people are more liberal, and they tend to vote Democrat." "What are you going to do with the gays?" "Will it be tough to draw Black people to your church?" Some would talk about the prevalence of homelessness.

What some saw as ministry-inhibitors, I viewed as ministry-enhancements. Some of the challenges were the very reason we were in the city. I envisioned a church that embraced individuals from all backgrounds, shades of skin, and across the political spectrum. My view of ministry was not to gather all those who think the same way, but to extend the welcome of Jesus to the hurting, broken, and confused, as well as the spiritually healthy. My vision was to take the simple message of God's redemption to a hurting world. My overriding objective has always been to point new friends to the one who turns mourning into joy.

Many churches today, to their credit, are looking for ways to extend a welcome to those of a different shade of skin. Some churches recognize they are missing out by not including their neighbors who may not look exactly like them. Christian Church Buckhead (CCB) has not had to deal with this because a foundational value from the very beginning was that every person is a child of God, created in his image, and designed for fellowship with him.

My first wedding as pastor of CCB was for Derrick, who is Black, and Lauren, who is white. It was a beautiful ceremony, and I celebrated our first wedding in Buckhead, reflecting our natural diversity. The priority of that value has continued as the church has grown and attracted individuals and families from many cultural backgrounds.

I am so blessed as I look back and reflect on the experience of planting this new church. No matter how focused or driven a leader is, we all dread criticism or someone questioning our motives. I want everyone to be happy, to agree with the vision, and to be supportive. It was tough to deal with people I care about as they presented all the challenges to me, because it sent strong, negative vibes into my spirit. I had to resist them. I was laser-focused on getting this new church off to a solid beginning.

More troubling was hearing Christian friends, even ministers, blatantly disparage whole groups of people (liberals, gay people, Black people, and the wealthy) with bigoted characterizations. Painful to me was the revelation these comments uncovered the theology of some dear friends. It seemed they did not believe the love of God extended to people who didn't look like them. Or, they did not believe anyone needed to take the message of God's love into the city. Or, they did not believe God would provide the resources for this new work. Or, they operated from a place of fear rather than faith.

Perhaps they simply didn't preach the gospel! Many of the reactions were extremely disappointing.

However, the positive responses to our vision of starting a church in the city were extensive and more than balanced the naysayers. So many people celebrated our bold move into the heart of Atlanta, the unofficial capital of the southeast region. So many Christ-followers from different denominations sent notes of encouragement. Business leaders in the area were glad we were doing something with that "eyesore" on Piedmont Road, and I was welcomed into the Buckhead Business Association as a leader who was contributing to the overall success of the area. Non-churched individuals gave me positive feedback because, I think, they understood the idea of transforming the building into something useful and productive.

I also received many emails and affirmations from ministers in the Atlanta metro area as well as nationally. Once the Associated Press picked up the story, I heard from friends all over the country and around the world. All were encouraging, and most of them really understood what we were trying to do with this unique venue.

While starting a church from scratch felt like a leap off the cliff … into the lake … at night, I knew I was not alone. God was with me every step of the way. I had churches which believed in us, prayed, and financially supported. And I was blessed with many friends who stood by me all the way.

Dan M. Garrett

CHAPTER FOUR:

"Do You Want to Make a Difference in the World?"

Raising financial support is always a challenge, but this endeavor proved to be an extreme sport. With most typical church plants, there is a "mother" church close by who sends people and money to get the project off the ground until it becomes self-supporting. In almost every way, we were not a "typical" church plant. I had no sponsoring church. I was the only member at the beginning. I joked that my wife waited to see what kind of worship music we had before she decided to join!

I spent ten months planning this new church. Much of that time involved contacting organizations, churches, and individuals, soliciting donations to our dream with one question: Do you want to make a difference in the world?

I aligned with Stadia, a national church-planting ministry, one year prior to planting, as they were experts in details such as an extensive timeline of what needed to happen and when.

As we move through life, we have no idea how relationships can come back to bless us in the future. Our project received incredible financial and human resourcing support from area churches, and most of these came because of friendships built through many years. The church I served for eleven years, Mount Carmel Christian Church, was an early supporter. Key supporting churches included: Heritage Church and their minister Greg Marksberry, who became a wise confidant and valued friend; Stephen Carpenter and Christ's Church at Whitewater; Spring Road Christian Church; Paul Leslie and McDonough Christian; Chris Stovall and LifePoint: Barry McCarty at Roswell First Christian; and North Druid Hills Christian Church.

I remember speaking at Roswell Christian Church, and Elder Bennie Slone spoke a beautiful blessing, "Buckhead is known as the life of the city. We pray for Christian Church Buckhead as they introduce eternal life to those in the city."

Another special gift from God came in the person of Dr. Marlin Day. When we met, he was the retired pastor and served as the unpaid leader of the small remnant of folks worshiping at North Druid Hills Christian Church, which he had started in one of the historic districts of Atlanta many years prior. He had seen the church grow and then decline as neighborhood demographics changed, while the church's outreach had not. Dr. Day was also the Chief Chaplain for the Atlanta Veterans Administration Medical Center.

Dr. Day heard about my goal of starting a church in Buckhead. He called and offered us free office space in their church building. I quickly accepted his gracious gift. Our small core group was eager to have a place to call our own, especially at no charge. We met for worship occasionally with the twenty senior adults who still called North Druid Hills Church home.

After a couple of months, Dr. Day asked me to meet him at McDonald's for breakfast. As we chatted over coffee, he got to the point of the meeting.

"Dan, we are ready to close the church. The land is worth quite a bit. Would you be okay if we sold the building and gave your church plant a million dollars?"

I'm not often at a loss for words; actually, I'm NEVER at a loss for words. But that day–I sat in silence. I felt like God was confirming the vision for a new church in the city. I finally managed to mumble a "yes" and "thank you."

Dr. Day said there would be some steps to the process, but he was confident the remaining members were positive about the dream for Buckhead. As things usually go, there were other opinions about how to divide the proceeds from the sale. A para-church organization came into the mix. When things settled out, the North Druid Hills Church decided to grant money to a number of area ministries, such as Atlanta Christian College and Woodland camp. Christian Church Buckhead eventually received $100,000, for which we were extremely grateful (but also slightly disappointed).

We still had to raise a ton of money to pull this venture together.

I made phone calls, set up meetings, and sent emails and letters. This was a top priority six days a week. I know my friends had to grow weary of my fundraising and probably dreaded seeing my number pop up on their phones! Sometimes, instead of saying hello, they would just answer, "I'm broke!" Many of them also said, "You're the most expensive friend I have."

After ten months of fundraising, we had $300,000 to get us launched. That may sound like a good number, and I did thank God for it, but it was not enough to keep us going. We had three full-time employees, which included an associate pastor and children's minister and three part-time staff, which was the worship minister, teen minister, and administrative assistant. That was the church-planting model in those days, called a parachute plant. Raise big money, hire your staff, and offer a fully functioning church from day one. (At least, that was how it worked in theory.)

I continued to solicit individuals and churches for funding. While I have always had to raise money for various projects throughout my ministry, this one was daunting. As pastor of

Spring Road Church, I had designed and spearheaded the funding campaign as we built a first-class, multipurpose center, including a gym, meeting hall, classrooms, and kitchen at a cost of $3 million. The difference was I led an established congregation there, with many affluent givers. The Buckhead project needed close to one million dollars, with our only sources of revenue being a few churches and no real members of the church, just those checking it out and most not quite ready to commit.

I leaned on the Lord for assurance, comfort, and hope. He came through. Almost every day, a check would come in the mail. Sometimes, these were from acquaintances, but often they were from people none of us even knew. On opening day, a couple dropped a check in the offering plate for $5,000. The money kept coming, and I decided I could not stress over this. I had to trust the Lord to provide while I kept devoting time to leading and developing our new fledgling church family.

CHAPTER FIVE:

From Gold Club to God's Club

I spent almost a year in preparation for planting this church. There were many aspects of laying the foundation before opening the doors. And besides, we didn't have any doors to open!

As part of the church-planting group we were associated with, Carol and I were expected to attend a week of leader training. Most of the planters attending were in their twenties. With twenty-five years of ministry under my belt, and at age forty-seven, I was surely the oldest living church-planter in captivity! But we knew this was important, so we jumped right in. We gained some valuable insights and quickly realized church planting is not for the weak or easily intimidated.

During 2003, my weeks consisted of making phone calls and having meetings to raise funds and share the vision. I met with pastors all around the metro Atlanta area, explaining the need for a church in Buckhead and asking for their financial and prayer support. It was a necessary task and one I enjoyed as I spent time with men and women I respect and consider to be brothers and sisters.

The rest of my time was consumed with designing a marketing strategy, seeking out and interviewing potential staff, and planning the first year's calendar. The biggest challenge hanging over me was finding a venue.

To be clear, prayer was a major component of the pre-planning. I took the biblical encouragement to "pray without ceasing" as a personal mandate. Nothing of any significance would happen apart from the power of God supplying all that was needed.

I personally started and ended every day with prayer.

Prayer was also a top priority with our launch team. We called our group of about twenty people committed to helping plant the church our P.R.E.P. team.

Pray … for God's will to be done and for his power to be released.

Recruit … others to be involved with us and invite friends to the church.

Equip … our team with skills to carry out the tasks.

Prepare … for February 2004 kick-off.

I have taught for many years that, when you dream a God-sized dream, all sorts of forces will emerge which seem intent on crushing your dreams and vision. I had warned the PREP team to be ready to experience discouragement and pushback from all sorts of places. Sometimes this evidences itself through sickness, sometimes through disparaging remarks from acquaintances, and sometimes just presenting as internal doubt.

The answer to negativity and questioning is always to pray, to seek the One who calms our spirits and infuses us with hope, truth, and peace.

One of the biggest challenges to our dream was finding a meeting space. We had set a target date of February 4 to launch. Super Bowl Sunday seemed like a good way to tie in "kicking off" a new thing. But, it was now September, time was ticking away, and we still did not have a location secured where we could meet every week.

I started a notepad of venue possibilities. Atlanta History Center (a prominent location that featured an excellent amphitheater room with stage and state-of-the-art sound), AMC Theatres (in the upscale Phipps Shopping Plaza), Oglethorpe University, and about twenty-five other potential locations appeared on my list. I was looking for a venue that would attract young urban professionals, my targeted demographic.

One afternoon, my wife Carol and I were in the slightly run-down part of Buckhead, driving up Piedmont Road and passed the Gold Club, a sad, lonely looking building painted completely black with a gold awning protruding from the entrance. Grass and weeds grew in the cracks in the unused parking lot. Surrounded by streets on all sides, it sat there all alone. A couple of chains blocked the two parking lot entrances. Carol suggested, "Why not rent the Gold Club?"

I laughed. (I laugh all the time, and just about everything seems funny to me.) This really seemed funny … until I looked over at Carol and she wasn't laughing. *I guess she doesn't understand how crazy an idea this is. Good grief, she's serious.*

I turned and asked, "The Gold Club? America's most 'infamous' strip club? For my new church?"

She simply responded, "Yes, and you can even rename it God's Club!"

I kept driving … and thinking … and driving … and praying a little. Considering that Carol seemed to be focused on this, and not wanting to ignore a possible idea that could have come from the Lord, I decided to check it out. Why not? Everything was a possibility at this point.

So I made a few calls and discovered the building was owned by a prominent developer in Atlanta, Kim King. I soon arranged a time with his office to check out the building.

I immediately called my good friend Wayne Leslie, a super-successful developer and contractor, having built Home

Depot and Kroger buildings all over the Southeast. He was one of the first persons I met when I moved to Atlanta long ago and has been a treasured friend for many years. I knew he would give me an honest perspective on whether we could do anything with this nasty old building.

A realtor from King's office met me and Wayne at the club. We unlocked the big, heavy metal door on the side of the building and walked into a stairwell. We could only see a few feet ahead as the power was turned off, and no lighting was available. It was difficult to get a grasp of the scope of the potential project. Wayne shone his flashlight around and mumbled to himself about needing to knock down that wall and fix that wiring, etc. I was just eager to have him pronounce that this was either workable or not worth considering.

We exited the building and discussed the situation. He kept saying there were so many things he couldn't really see in the darkened building and wasn't sure about some of the important aspects such as leaks, wiring, and other potential problems.

I remember surprising myself with the enthusiasm building within me for this cruddy, square block structure. I truly attribute this to God's Spirit. There were a ton of reasons why birthing our church in a former strip club was a stupid idea. I was smart enough to know this would alienate a large chunk of the people we wanted to attract. Whether you label it as "snobby" or not, this whole scenario was not going to be a place many "Buckheaders" would want to go for church. But, I felt strongly that "God's Club" would send a clear signal— God loves all kinds of people, and every person matters in spite of what they have done. I said often, "When you have a church in an old strip club, it pretty much sends a message that everyone is welcome here!"

So, I kept pressing Wayne for an answer. He was the expert contractor, and if he said "don't do it," I definitely would not have kept moving forward. He looked at me and said, "Do you know how many crazy things you have gotten me into?" (I won't go into the reason he said that right now. I'll save that for another book! Ha!)

Wayne let out a long sigh and smiled. "Dan, I think this is going to be a giant project, and there will be all kinds of problems we haven't anticipated. I'm very concerned about the wiring mess in this building. I have no idea if the heat works, and it will be nearly impossible to get all the permits in time for you to meet your grand opening date. But … I know you, and if anyone can pull this off, it's you. And … it sure seems like God is in this, so I know it will work. I say it's a GO."

Wow! Wayne thinks this can work! (Typical of me, I sort of ignored all his hesitations and concerns and focused on the fact that he said it's doable.) Then, he said, "I'm going to donate one of my supervisors to be on site throughout the renovation. He will be able to guide your volunteers and provide expert advice. And I will send equipment and materials." *Wow again!*

Thank you, Lord, for providing for this project before it even started. And thank you, Lord, for my friend Wayne.

I called the building owner, and we discussed next steps for leasing the Gold Club. A few days later, we scheduled a big meeting in Kim King's boardroom on the top floor of his beautiful office complex he had constructed across from Georgia Tech University. The meeting room was dominated by a long, shiny table, and the walls were covered with framed photos of the many buildings constructed by Mr. King's company.

The meeting turned out to be pretty funny. (But, remember, I think most everything has some humor in it.) Along one side of the important looking table were seated Mr. King, his son, his brother, and his attorney. On our side of the table ... me and my young associate, Chris Smith, a Georgia Tech graduate and newly graduated from Emmanuel Theological Seminary. Both groups looked over the lease agreement, briefly discussed a couple of items, and then we were ready to discuss lease rate. Mr. King's attorney began by noting the monthly loan payment they were making was $26,000, and that was the amount they would need.

I visibly winced.

The attorney continued, rather emphatically, as if defending that astounding lease cost, "The current rate of lease for this type of building…"

I interrupted, with some notable sarcasm, "You have comparable lease rates for an abandoned strip club? A block building with no windows, painted totally black and sitting empty for three years?"

Everyone sat quietly for a minute, I believe while acknowledging the obvious absurdity of the King group bringing up comps. The attorney reiterated, "Our payment is $26,000."

My response was simple and straightforward, "Your loan payment has no connection with the value of the property in terms of its lease potential."

They knew I was right, but they weren't prepared to deal with a pastor who knew how things worked in real life. Mr. King nodded to his team, and we moved forward.

Fairly quickly we came to an agreement for half that amount as our monthly lease. It was still exorbitant, but it was Buckhead, and that's where we were called to plant our church.

As we were ready to sign the documents, Kim King's son, Beau, shuffled in his chair and began a question. I say "began," because he seemed to be uncomfortable as he tried to ask it. I wasn't sure he was ever going to finish. "Dan, you know … our company's name is associated with this project … and, umm … we are glad you will be leasing the building, but … well, we don't want anything … umm …"

I interrupted Beau. (Mainly because I was ready for lunch!) I said, "You are wondering if we are a crazy church and might embarrass your company, right?" Beau sort of embarrassingly nodded. I leaned forward and said, "Well, let me assure you, we will not be handling snakes that first Sunday!"

Everyone paused. I flashed a big grin, and then the whole group burst out laughing. The owners of the building just needed to know we were "safe." We agreed on lease terms and signed the papers. We were now the proud renters of an ugly, square box located in the middle of the most questionable section of Buckhead. And, to think we leased the place after only walking through with a pitiful flashlight for a few minutes.

What in the world have I done?

CHAPTER SIX:

A Moment of Silence

ere we go. I unlocked the door to the closed-down Gold Club and turned on the lights. There were ten of us—a few college students, a couple in their fifties, and a few young adults. We just stood quietly. No one wanted to speak. All of us experienced a wave of emotions. We stood in the dressing room for the dancers, and it was awkward, sad, enlightening, and slightly overwhelming all at the same time.

When the feds closed the club, they arrested the manager, ran everyone out, and padlocked the building. For four years, no one had even stepped inside. Some realtors purchased the building from the government, but had not done anything with the property. It took us a few days to get the electricity turned on so we could get started with the renovation. We really had no idea what to expect.

As I imagine it is for most people, my perception of strip clubs and the women who worked there was formed by the movies. Television shows and Hollywood often portray stripping as exotic and the ladies who participate as mysterious and glamorous. My encounter with the dressing room changed all that.

I don't know what we thought we were going to find as we entered a closed-down strip club, but this was definitely not it. In our minds, we were probably conjuring up movie scenes with lights flashing, mirrors, tables and chairs, liquor bottles laying around, and of course, a fancy stage with poles. Where we stood was just a few feet from the stage, but it was light years away otherwise.

We entered the dressing room, turned on the lights, and found ourselves staring at faces ... hundreds of faces on cabinet doors. Most of the doors hung open and they were covered with photographs. Yes, these were photos of "strippers," but they look like real people, not dressed up dancers who take off their clothes for inebriated men in a smoky room. Taped to the cabinet doors were photographs of mothers, aunts, daughters, sisters. Olan Mills pictures—with husbands, children, and even Santa for heaven's sake. Santa at the Gold Club!

My mind reeled. *Who are these people?*

Everyone in the business refers to the women who strip as "girls" or they call them dancers. But this scene challenged all the labels. These weren't "girls" or children. The people in these pictures were wives, mothers, partners ... women. These were not strippers. These were human beings. The pictures revealed a variety of individuals, with personalities, homes, and families. Just people.

Why did they tape these photos to their dressing room doors? My guess is to maintain a connection to reality. The photos reminded each dancer who they really were.

In theology, this view of humanity is based in Imago Dei, a term that suggests every individual is made in the image of God and therefore has inherent worth. This was the first of many truths to be highlighted in our minds and hearts through the process of cleaning out this formerly bustling business and turning it into a place of worship. Quit judging before you know the person. Every single human matters.

Stereotyping is built on ignorance. I allowed the media, and perhaps my own judgmental attitude, to form my ideas regarding the individuals who, for whatever reason, had chosen to take off their clothes to entertain men and make a living. Lesson number one: every human being is deserving of being treated with dignity, and should not be labeled and stereotyped.

Stereotyping lesson number two: we are not so different. These ladies were individuals who made bad choices. I make bad choices, too. Club dancers are persons who may have felt forced into a job they didn't want due to financial pressures. How many of us can relate to that as well?

Stereotyping lesson number three: pre-judging blocks us from relationships and understanding. If I decide *ahead of time* that certain groups of people are below me, inferior, and not worth dealing with, then I have robbed myself of potential wisdom, resources, friendships, and help. If I pre-determine, before I have any facts, then I have limited myself.

We tend to view addicts or sexual strugglers or alcoholics as uniquely different—we tend to believe it's who they inherently are. Or we see them as weaker than the rest of us. The irony is that we all have our own issues, but some struggles are public, and some are private or hidden. The fact is I'm less likely to stereotype others when I understand myself.

Stereotyping is dangerous as it categorizes and condemns whole groups of people. The truth is "they" are not so different from "us." Everyone seeks similar answers; we are all looking for meaning in life; we all need hope, laughter, and friends.

Understanding that humans are not much different from one another leads us to be givers of grace instead of pronouncers of worth.

Our clean-up team stood in silence in the locker room because important parts of our spirits were being awakened. We paused and contemplated, and I think for a few moments, we simply stood in honor. We recognized the shared humanity represented in those photos. And we left the locker room untouched physically, although our hearts were forever touched. It was the last area we cleaned out and fixed up. The ladies at least deserved that.

CHAPTER SEVEN:

From Poles to Pews

*H*ow am I going to let people know we are starting a *new church?* This marketing question haunted me more than even the fundraising. How would I break through the noise of the media to promote this exciting, new venture? I knew we would not have the kind of financial capacity to advertise in a big way and get the attention of Buckhead residents.

I should have known that God was way ahead of me, and I also should have trusted that my biggest mountain would be conquered with just a little faith.

The *Atlanta Journal-Constitution,* the primary newspaper for the metro area, picked up the story soon after we rented the facility, and we appeared on the front page of the Metro section. The article gave an overview of this enthusiastic group seeking to redeem the building and the city. For a couple of days, I received about a hundred phone calls from friends and others. Some questioned my sanity, while many were supportive, and others simply were intrigued by it all.

One article talked about a house of sin becoming a house of worship. Another said, where dancers once undressed, church folk will now be blessed.

The next day, the Associated Press took the story national, actually global. *CNN Headline News* began running coverage. Famed national radio commentator Paul Harvey mentioned us on his program. Now, I was hearing from people all over the world. The overall consensus was: this is so cool!

Our church had yet to launch, and we showed up on the front page of the Atlanta paper twice. Then, we became the topic of local talk radio. Our church's story appeared in newspapers around the nation, including the *Washington Post, New York Times* and *USA Today*. Two local television stations interviewed me. People said they saw us on Fox national tv, heard us on the local radio stations, and read about us in newspapers in Seattle, Dallas, and Miami.

We showed up online as well at CNN.com, Foxnews.com, Yahoo.com's unusual stories and even in Adult Industry News.

Whenever I was interviewed, I said this, "We're going to take something that was a mess and turn it into something good and usable." I took every opportunity to explain that God is eager and able to transform our lives just as we are renovating this deteriorating building.

One day, my wife called me. "Turn on WSB. I'm getting ready to be on Kim's show." I was thrilled. The number one afternoon radio show in metro Atlanta was the Kim Peterson show, which was a mix of comedy, skits, heated political arguments, listener call-ins, and more. Everybody listened on their way home from work. Carol had a connection with Kim as she was marketing director for a company that was one of the largest sponsors of his show.

Carol called in, and Kim immediately put her on air and began talking about our church leasing the old Gold Club. He loved it! He went right into the jokes. "Is your husband going to slide down the pole to preach? I wonder how the choir ladies will dress? How will you collect the offering, tuck the dollar bills in the usher's belts?"

Oh no. What began as excitement as I anticipated more publicity for our church, now turned to panic. I know how Kim's humor works. He will get on one topic and use it as a running gag for weeks. *This could be a disaster.*

But it wasn't. Kim kept Carol on the line for a whole segment, asked a ton of questions, and made a bunch of jokes. But then, as he wrapped up, he took a more serious tone. "I hope it goes great. I hope you have hundreds of people. Good luck."

Wow. Dan, breathe out. "Thank you, Lord," I whispered.

Fortunately, the remainder of our marketing took on a more strategic approach. Someone connected me with a gentleman named Rick Smith who does public relations. I discovered that Rick was well regarded among his many media contacts and was considered a rising star in the public relations world. I was fortunate to have him consider assisting us with getting our message out.

Rick is African-American and loved how the church's DNA from the beginning embraced diversity. He became one of our biggest fans, a great friend, and sounding board for me and my crazy ideas, and he and his wonderful family often worshiped with us. I attribute much of our success to Rick's skill and passion. He lined up various local newspapers to cover the story, arranged for television coverage, and coordinated interviews for me in several magazines and other print media.

It was now December. This ride was picking up speed, and it was about to get crazy.

Dan M. Garrett

CHAPTER EIGHT:

"We've Got Eight Weeks Until Opening Day!"

Y ou've got to clean out the old before you can bring in the new.

This is basic "gospel" teaching. We've got to wrestle with the bad news before we can grasp the Good News. Dealing with the reality of our own personal ugliness and sin helps us understand our desperate situation of being separated from the One who can return us to our intended status of wholeness, a life filled with joy, purpose, and meaning.

It was impossible to renovate the building without doing some serious clean-out. We filled nine industrial dumpsters with junk, old sofas, rotting carpet, mirrors, old lockers, and a ton of other things nobody wanted! In fact, the place was so nasty, that all of us working joked that we would not bend down and pick up anything less than a $20 bill! We even had a $10 bill someone had swept up tacked to the bulletin board. Nobody wanted it because it was so gross, although it did eventually disappear.

We started out trying to take down the seemingly endless mirrors which covered the walls. They were everywhere. We finally decided a wiser and safer plan was to cover the mirrors rather than bust them out. A group from my former church in Alabama (Spring Road) came to help, and one gentleman arranged to get giant bolts of curtain material donated by WestPoint Stevens. Curtains were then hung by that team. Another friend of mine from the church I had served in Decatur made a call to a buddy in north Georgia, and carpet was delivered at no cost. Someone (I don't even know who) gave us office furniture.

The message of transformation resonated. Helpers from around Atlanta just started showing up. Fred, a bearded gentleman in his sixties, who later told us he was a Presbyterian, simply arrived one morning with his table saw and set up an area to cut pieces of wood for all the mini-projects taking place all over the building. He came every day for two weeks.

Individuals from various religious tribes joined him in the work: singles from Hebron Baptist Church, along with motivated servants from the Assembly of God, a couple of Methodist churches, and many others. Most volunteers brought tools. And all came with the same enthusiasm for redeeming the "den of iniquity." A short-term mission team from Indiana worked with us for a week. (I'm still not sure how they heard about us!)

John Vernon, minister and director of the Jesus Place homeless ministry in downtown Atlanta showed up with some of his men to help tear out walls and remove debris. What a picture of servanthood this was—men who struggled with addictions and mental illness, and who depended on the kindness of others for clothes and meals, enthusiastically hauled trash and helped with demolition to transform an old building into a place of worship. Wow!

This was an incredible illustration of the body of Christ at work as we used our gifts for a common purpose: to revitalize a dilapidated building in preparation for reaching others with a simple message of grace.

Every workday at the project began with prayer. Men and women of all ages, plus teenagers and Georgia Tech students, would join hands and stand in a circle. The prayers did not all sound the same, but there was a richness to this that cannot be explained, only experienced. The big clean out was a God-thing from beginning to end. We could not have done this on our own.

I came in one evening, and there was a man, maybe in his twenties, on his knees, spreading something on the concrete floor of what would be the main seating area. I asked one of our volunteers, "Who is this guy?"

"Oh, that's my cousin. He lays carpet. He's doing this for free. He thinks what we are doing is so cool."

I replied, "Well, that is a blessing. He sure seems to be working super-fast."

The volunteer replied, "Yeah, he's a cocaine addict, and he plans on being here all night and having the carpet all laid by the morning."

Well, okay then.

From the beginning of this process, I had been told that getting the building inspected and approved by our goal date was 99 percent impossible. Those in the know assured me that city inspectors can be difficult to work with, and the permitting process can be cumbersome and challenging.

So we prayed. And we prepared.

When the first electrical inspector showed up, he laughed. We had so much that had to be done to come up to code. The building had sat empty for four years. Instead of fighting with him, we listened, asked what we needed to do to be able to open in six weeks, and we showered him with kindness! (And, unknown to him, we had a group of people praying for him and for his decision-making.)

He said, "I don't usually do this, but I will come back in two weeks, instead of two months, and if everything is as it should be, we should be good to go."

We thanked him, and we got busy getting that electrical up to speed.

Water was a whole different story. The inspectors came a few times and kept holding up our certificate of occupancy. We finally received permission to open three days before Kick-off Sunday.

My old friend from Mount Carmel days owns a painting company. He brought his crew, and they painted the whole outside of the building for free. Incredible! They turned that old, ugly, black box into a welcoming space and a powerful marketing tool, as thousands of cars passed by there every day.

Another Mount Carmel youth grouper, Ward Jenkins, a professional artist, painted our church logo on the wall of the building facing Piedmont Road.

One of my favorite things that happened throughout the renovation project was when someone would come into the building to speak with me. We were incredibly busy, but I was very conscious of appreciating those who came to help, those who stopped in to say hello, and others who were just curious. But almost everyone asked the same question, and made the same joke: Are you going to slide down the pole to preach?

So, I got one of those clickers you hold in your hand, the kind they use at Six Flags Park to count customers. I kept the clicker in my pocket and pulled it out every time someone asked me that question, which they thought was so original. I would say: "Gosh, you're the 235th person who thinks that's funny!" (Sorry, I have the spiritual gift of sarcasm!)

My other favorite thing to do was to kid with the guys who came into our renovating project. Most were friends from Atlanta stopping in to check things out. I would say, kind of softly, "Listen, I came across this file cabinet with names of customers and found some receipts with your name on it. You know, I need to raise a lot of money to get this venture off the ground, and I can make that file go away for a donation!"

The guy would take a second, then laugh, and say, "I've never been in here." And we would all have a good laugh.

But one time I pulled this joke, and the man got all attitude with me and huffed, "You didn't find my name, I've never stepped foot in here. That's crazy." (This response made me think he probably had stepped foot in there.) Anyway, it was fun to mess with people! Most had fun with the whole joke.

When you need some walls built for kid's Sunday school classes, it doesn't matter if the guy cutting the wood is Southern Baptist or Pentecostal. God's people working together can yield great results.

Lesson Learned:

You've got to clean out the old before you can bring in the new.

CHAPTER NINE:

"We've Been Expecting You!"

It didn't take me long to figure out this whole God's Club adventure was not really my idea. Just as the Pilgrims landed and the Native Americans welcomed them with a little dinner and the obvious news that they had not "discovered" anything, I learned that God had been at work on Piedmont Road for quite a while.

A variety of individuals stopped by to share their story with me. There was a common thread—they had all been praying for God to do something with the empty Gold Club.

A distinguished looking "Buckhead lady" (meaning she was dressed tastefully, with impressive jewelry) stopped by the office one day and asked to see the pastor. Seeming to be in her late sixties, Mrs. Turner delightfully relayed to me that she and a few other women were involved in a weekly Bible study group, and part of their prayer time for the last two years included asking the Lord to do something positive with that old club. How awesome and humbling this was to me.

A Black woman, about thirty years old, came up to me as I was leaving the project one day. She laughed as she explained how she worked in town, but somehow took a wrong turn one New Year's Eve going to her office party. As she drove by the club, right around midnight, she felt compelled to pull in. She sat in her car, prayed, and "claimed this corner" for God. In my younger days as a minister, I might have dismissed this narrative, but my perspective has certainly changed as I have seen God at work in various times and places. My job is not to analyze, but to listen and respond!

One day we were painting one of the children's ministry rooms and I was getting a little discouraged about whether we could truly pull this whole thing off. A man tapped me on the shoulder and said, "I have been praying against this place for a long time, and a friend at work told me it was now a church and I couldn't believe it. I just had to come see for myself." He informed me that about a year ago, he laid hands on the building and asked God for a miracle. I barely had time to absorb his comments when one of the volunteer workers needed my attention. After a brief conversation, I turned around and my visitor was gone. When I quizzed those standing around about the man, no one had seen him. (Hmmm. An angel sent at just the right time?)

I had more than a few individuals tell me they prayed for that corner as they would sit at the red light. Isn't that so cool to think about? While surrounded by cars, city noise, the stress of the day, and the choice of listening to music, someone chooses to spend that minute at the light to ask God to do something big with a nasty old former strip club. That's awesome!

These stories, coming from persons of varying ages, economic status, and shades of skin, served as incredible affirmations that God was doing a good thing and we were invited into it. The feeling is like that of an athlete when everything comes together and you find your "zone," knowing you are in the right place at the right time.

I knew all along starting a church in the city would be larger than I could pull off on my own. But God kept sending signals that I was not in this alone. He sent young people with energy. He sent older adventurers, like Jeff and Laura Kern, to share their wisdom and calm strength. He sent messages that others had been praying for this. He sent finances through friends, churches, and organizations. He sent my good friend and contractor to help guide the renovation, and he brought me a team of staff members to help pull this all together. The task was almost overwhelming until I stopped, in humility, and thanked God this project belonged to him and not me.

For twelve months, since launching into this incredible journey, I began every day before I got out of bed by praying, "Lord, this project is so big and I don't know if I'm up to the task, but this is your church and not mine. Thank you for letting me be a part of it." And I went to bed each night, praying, "Lord, I did my best today, and I'm concerned about so many things, but I know the success is not dependent upon me. This is your church. I give it to you. Good night. Amen."

I prayed those prayers for two reasons. First, I truly did not know the secrets of growing a church in the city, and I needed God's power. Second, I could not bear all the responsibility for this; I had to give this to God, or I would not have been able to go to sleep each night. Christian Church Buckhead belonged to God. It was fun to rename the Gold Club to God's Club because it truly was his!

Lessons Learned:

God was at work here long before I showed up.

Great works of God are preceded by great seasons of prayer.

Dan M. Garrett

CHAPTER TEN:

"We Don't Have Enough Chairs!"

The final week before kick-off was crazy! I mean super crazy!

A few weeks prior, I was standing outside the building, and a rough looking truck turned into the parking lot, pulling a trailer full of washing machines and dryers. An older man, bearded and disheveled, got out, and we started chatting about my project of starting a church in the Gold Club. He laughed and told me he had just bought all the items in the Holiday Inn just down the street which was soon to be torn down. "What do you need?"

"Man, I need chairs. I've got no chairs. Oh, and I need two toilets."

The junk man replied, "You are in luck. I've got about a hundred cloth chairs, and I have a couple of toilets right here on the trailer."

I was thrilled and asked, "How much?"

He paused and looked up. Right above where we were standing in front of the building were large mounted letters spelling out The Gold Club, all in neon.

My new friend asked, "What are you going to do with that big neon sign? Those can be worth a good amount. I will trade you the toilets and the chairs for the sign."

The owners had told me from the beginning that they didn't care what I did with the building or the furnishings. Their intent was to tear it down and build a condo tower, so I felt free to negotiate the neon signs.

I didn't hesitate. "You've got a deal. But you must take it down."

The junk man said he would bring me the chairs soon, and take the sign.

My first thought was—Man, I'm proud of myself as a negotiator! I just took care of two big concerns, and it didn't really cost me a dime.

My second thought was—I can't believe I went to Bible College and seminary, and I'm out on Piedmont Road wheeling and dealing for toilets and old chairs for my strip club church.

Two weeks before kick-off and no chairs.

I called the junk man, who mumbled, "Oh yeah, I will be there tomorrow."

A week goes by—no chairs. I called the junk man.

He said, "I'm coming tomorrow."

And he did. With fifty chairs.

Now I was stressed. "Dude, where are the other chairs?"

The junk man responded with his favorite answer, "I will bring them tomorrow." He didn't.

We were one week out. We had no water, no heat, no working men's room, and not enough chairs!

I called the junk man every day. Nothing.

The chairs he had brought were rough. Some had cigarette burns. Most had stains. All smelled bad.

We were to open in three days. Thankfully, the water now worked, as did both restrooms. The heat was temperamental and worked occasionally. It was February and cold!

Friday, we rented a cleaning machine from Home Depot, and a few of the Georgia Tech students started washing and scrubbing chairs. They had fun, and it seemed like two days would be enough time for the chairs to dry. Things moved along, but I still needed the other fifty chairs. We planned on having two worship services, with about 100 people at each.

On Saturday, we arrived early and stayed late. Lots of volunteers worked, straightening, folding information flyers, setting up children's rooms, and a hundred other tasks.

All through the day, someone would yell out, "We open tomorrow!"

I was a little stressed, just wanting everything to be ready, but I sort of enjoyed the organized chaos. People had fun, hurrying to get their particular area ready, but kidding around and even stopping occasionally to pray with each other.

The welcome team set up the tent just outside the main entrance doors, where refreshments would be served.

Inside, my wife, Carol, and my kids, vacuumed, swept, and dusted.

Even with multiple vacuum cleaners making noise, the band practiced, working out bugs with the sound system. We had a sound team in the balcony running the mixer board.

At two o'clock in the afternoon, the junk man brought the remaining fifty chairs. More orange, nasty chairs, with cigarette burns and stains. At least we had chairs.

The college students unloaded the chairs. Too cold to take this project outside, they lined up the chairs in the lobby, sprayed them with a water and cleaner mix, and then scrubbed them with a brush. The chairs were then spread throughout the building to dry.

A couple of guys placed signs out by Piedmont Road, advertising church times. And they put up a wooden cross which could be seen by the thousands of cars passing by.

I moved from being stressed to fighting off panic. I had fifty wet chairs! *Good grief.*

I don't know when I got home that night, and I sure don't remember sleeping. Tomorrow was the big day, ready or not.

Dan M. Garrett

CHAPTER ELEVEN:

This Is Your House.

Super Bowl Sunday. Opening Day. When I pulled into the parking lot, cars were already there, as the band was inside setting up.

Other volunteers began to arrive. Smiles and laughter permeated everywhere.

We circled up and prayed. "Lord, this is your place, your ministry, your church. Thank you for every person who has worked to make this a welcoming space. May we bless the people you bring here today and in the future. In Jesus' name, Amen."

Most of us still talk about how cold the weather was outside and how warm the atmosphere stayed inside the building. It just felt like the Holy Spirit was present and pleased.

All three of Atlanta's major TV stations arrived and set up cameras in the balcony. Afterwards they walked around and interviewed some of our attendees and staff.

The sound booth team played music over the speakers as people arrived.

Guests parked and grabbed a coffee or hot chocolate, and maybe a donut, in the tent outside. Moving through the big glass entrance doors and into the lobby, each person was greeted by smiling college students and senior adults handing out programs.

People were clapping and smiling, and then Jamie and the band got worship started with some music. And they rocked the house. Everyone stood and sang enthusiastically.

The next tune brought the tempo down a little as powerful words were sung by our team, inviting the heavenly Father to come and dwell, making it clear that "this is your house."

Awesome words. I was tearful as I looked around the room at the more than 200 smiling faces, reflecting on all the renovation that had taken place, and just finally realizing the dream was coming true.

The whole group gathered that day seemed to sing in unison, "We dedicate this temple to you, Lord."

The worship team was leading us in songs about worshiping in a temple and singing praises in the sanctuary. We had come a long way from a darkened room filled with flashing lights and thumping music to a "sanctuary" whose walls now reflected healing and redemption.

Our prayer became, "Holy Spirit, overflow this place."

The song about "this is your house" became a theme for us. We used it for pre-service every week for a long time. I would often refer to these lyrics as I would teach. Sometimes, I would just start singing the song and the crowd would join in …This is your house, Father, come and dwell …

Our worship pastor, Jamie, has an awesome heart and a wonderful gift of playing and singing and leading others. We had worked together at the church in Alabama. While there, he had struggled with some sin and temptation and had stepped away from official paid ministry for a time. He did not think he would ever return to ministry. Now he was back—a magnificent illustration of God's leading, mercy, and timing— and, one more piece of the picture that CCB was becoming a place for imperfect people, the preacher and ministry staff included, serving a perfect God.

Jamie grew up in Atlanta and was able to recruit band members from his friend circles, students from Georgia Tech's campus ministry, and former youth groupers of churches he and I had served. He was brilliant in bringing together a diverse group and making incredible music.

One of the funny things about the band was that some of the musicians were playing in bars the night before, getting home in the middle of the night, or not going home at all, and heading straight to God's Club. They would show up on Sunday morning and give us their best, which was typically fantastic.

Following the worship songs, we served communion, which is a time of remembering the death of Christ by receiving a piece of bread and a small cup of juice. This important time, though brief, is the most significant part of the worship service. I think the most satisfying moment for me of that first Sunday, and for each week following, was watching the communion trays being passed down the rows and unlikely people marking God's grace in an unlikely place.

My first sermon in the "new" building reflected a central theme of my beliefs, formed over twenty-five years of study, teaching, and personal interaction with thousands of people. God's desire for his children is "Direction, not Perfection."

I held up a football and asked those gathered to picture the stage as a football field.

"We understand the goal in football is to move down the field and hopefully score a touchdown. Do this more than the other team, and you are the winner. Many of us operate from that metaphor as we go through life. You move forward eight yards, but get tackled and lose a few yards. It is easy to constantly measure my life based on my location on the field (of life) and basing success according to the amount of positive forward motion."

Acting out the highs and lows of making some yardage and then experiencing the setbacks helped me convey the continual frustration of figuring out what yard line I'm on and focusing on whether I am winning or losing.

"A better picture for understanding life and how we relate to God, is rafting." Holding up an oar, I stated, "Life is not a game to be won. It's not designed to be a football, constantly pressing for more yardages and scores. Life is a river. It moves fast and slow. There are rapids, and there are times to just float. Chaos and calm."

As the image of a flowing stream came onto the large screen, I continued, "The satisfying life is found in learning to navigate the twists and turns, occasionally pulling off and resting to enjoy the scenery. The goal is not to be the first across the finish line, but to enjoy the trip."

"It's easy to focus on winning and losing, but sanctification is the work of the Holy Spirit in your life–continually cleansing, redeeming, and shaping. Holiness is not **getting** there; it's **going** there.

I concluded my message by pointing out that the key to a rich and fulfilling life is to understand and live by the principle of direction, not perfection. The question we tend to ask is: "Have I arrived?" The better question is: "Am I headed the right way?"

As the message concluded, the applause encouraged me. It felt like we were in the right place doing the right things.

After the closing prayer, the band played while staff, volunteers, and the many guests hung out to talk, laugh, and celebrate an awesome beginning.

Because we anticipated a big crowd, we held a second service, which was equally meaningful and inspiring, with even more people. A grand total of 450 people were part of the Christian Church Buckhead kick-off. Thank you, Lord.

Later that day, we had a Super Bowl party in the building. The techie guys set up the big screen for all of us to watch the game. One TV station returned for our big party and interviewed me and others. This presented another opportunity for me to explain how God is in the business of transformation.

One last story about that first day. Jerry and Nancy, long-time friends, came up to me after the second service. Jerry was shaking his head and smiling. He reminded me that we had run into each other at a gathering about six months prior, and he asked me why I had moved back to Atlanta. He remembers me saying, "We are starting a church in Buckhead. We don't have any people and no building. We need to raise lots of money.

And I think we will have between 400 and 500 people on opening day."

Jerry held my arms and drew me in closer. "I thought you were crazy. I didn't know how you were going to do this, but here we are. You had 450 people here for the grand opening, you've raised a ton of money, and so many young people are involved. God is good."

Yes he is, Jerry. Yes he is.

Dan M. Garrett

CHAPTER TWELVE:

God's Plans Are Bigger Than Our Plans.

I had a certain idea of what this ministry was going to look like, a picture in my mind of meeting for worship in the Atlanta History Center and attracting young urban professionals. I envisioned navy jackets, a medium-range worship set, and then a nice lunch in a local bistro. But God's Club changed all that.

Our heavenly Father seemed to have a different story-line in his mind. I believe he saw a space serving as a reflection of the great diverse mix of individuals living in town. And that is exactly what was birthed at Christian Church Buckhead. We learned quickly when you open a church in a former strip club, you don't really need a sign which says: Everyone Welcome. The message is loud and clear: we're not "too good" for you.

Strugglers are welcomed here. I believe this is the message of scripture.

Buildings, spaces, and places can shape the people who gather there. The God's Club space set a tone. The building itself was part of the message—anyone can come in here. People got it … you don't need to have your stuff together before entering. And they came.

You don't manufacture diversity. It's organic. You don't force unity. It flows from each person recognizing the worth of the other. We do not embrace the concepts of diversity or unity as a "church growth" engine. These things are built into us in our very DNA. Respect for the "other" is an outgrowth of personal spiritual formation. This is the work of the Holy Spirit.

The higher, richer approach to diversity is grace. Grace tolerates—it doesn't demand instant change. Grace accepts. Grace acknowledges that every human being has inherent worth because we are all made in the image of God. Grace recognizes the reality that we are all messed up. Grace seeks the other's good.

The image of the church in our American culture as hateful and judgmental is not new. I wanted our church to change that perspective.

I was also convicted about breaking down the illusion that we had come to town to save people and fix the broken. Church people are broken, too. I shared with our planning team often that "We need to come in humility and simply point people to Jesus."

I felt strongly that we come in power, Holy Spirit power, to accomplish the mission. We love people the way God has loved us. Our message must always be, "While we were yet sinners, Christ died for us."

Our church family was a beautiful tapestry of personalities and socioeconomic backgrounds. Nothing better illustrates the vibrant mix of people and consistent sold-out faith in Jesus than meeting a few individuals who were part of this startup.

Just a few days into our clean-up adventure, in early November, a sort of questionable looking character came through the front doors.

Joerod was short in stature, unshaven and wearing what looked to be his only set of clothes, which were shabby and dirty.

Winsome and smiling, Joerod came in and picked up a broom and started helping. For those of us who had been in ministry a while, we were somewhat skeptical. People who live on the street develop a persona, a skill of winning you over before fleecing you.

I heard some on our team warning each other, "Watch out. He's just working us. This guy will help out for an hour and then ask for money. Watch the stuff, the computers and the purses."

Each day Joerod returned. As he warmed up to our team, we discovered he was alcoholic and homeless. But he never asked for money. Never.

We were wrong about Joerod. He simply wanted to belong.

On the second Sunday, after we officially opened, someone on staff lined up Joerod to help serve communion. My first thought was–*oh no, visitors*. I was very conscious in the early days of the message we were sending in terms of our identity. The culture of an organization is set in the beginning stages by the visible way things are done. As I sat and fretted over this humble man from the streets distributing the symbols reminding us of how God humbled himself and became a human to live among us and eventually die, God broke my heart.

I said to myself, "If this child of God can't serve the Lord's Supper, then who can?" (Besides, he surely knows his way around wine!)

Joerod was accepted and loved, and gradually became an equally valued member of the Buckhead family. We tried to help. He drifted in and out of things. But all along, he was not a "project." He was one of us, a member of the team.

As Joerod became more comfortable with us, he shared that it had been a long time since he had seen his eight-year-old son. The young man lived with his mother, Joerod's ex-wife, about forty-five minutes away. One of our great couples lined up a day and took Joe to see his son. They said it was one of the best things they had ever done.

A number of other colorful characters entered the God's Club doors. Some stayed a few weeks or months, others disappeared after one Sunday, and many continue as members twenty years later.

- Street people like cowboy Jim and Guitar Pete.
- The general manager of the top radio station in Atlanta.
- A few widows.
- A lady who had been divorced a few times.
- Michael, a cocaine addict from New Jersey, whose father was in the New York Mafia. I remember him serving me communion one week.
- A few folks struggling with addictions.
- A dozen senior adults from the North Druid Hills church, all over seventy years old.
- A terrific young man named Adam, who was waiting on a kidney transplant, and was part of our sound team.

- A policeman and his family.

- Former dancers at the club.

- Men who were former patrons of the club.

- Several men and women who were gay.

- Atlanta Christian college students.

- A young man who was a recovering alcoholic. I'm sure there were more.

- A writer and on-air personality with CNN.

- People who had been away from the church.

So many fun and unique individuals became part of our story. One such person, whom absolutely everyone came to know, was Flash. He had been a comedy writer for Atlanta morning radio shows before developing multiple sclerosis. He called himself an agnostic but was intrigued when he received our postcard in the mail.

When Flash first visited, I asked him how he knew about us. "I got your mailer, and it said this church met at Phipps theaters. Well, that's my favorite place to go, so even though I'm not interested in church, I thought I need to go check out this church that meets in a theater."

Flash kept coming, made friends, was baptized, and joined a small group. Even as his MS disease diminished his physical abilities, his spiritual life increased.

Ileana, a single lady in her mid-twenties, became our first baptism.

Dr. Coby and Dr. Janet, a married couple with small children, were invited by a coworker and are still members today. When they told me they were both behavioral psychologists, I replied, "Well, I will keep you busy just figuring me out."

Marla, a vibrant, young lady who began attending at the invitation of a friend, dove right into volunteering and became a vital part of the leadership team. One Sunday morning she came in distraught, and soon her story had passed around the early set-up team. Marla had hired a contractor to renovate her kitchen and he swindled her out of $3,000 and left town.

That morning, in worship, we told her story and spontaneously took up an offering to help out. Three men from the church went that week and finished the project.

Everyone had fun being a part of this. The rest of the story is that her parents, out of gratitude, sent an end-of-the-year offering check that was three times what we had collected for their daughter.

A unique member of our family was Phil, who had moved to Atlanta from Boston to get away from the cult he was involved in. One Sunday morning, Phil took the metro train to learn the route to the new job he would be starting the next day. When he exited the station, he saw our sign and came in … and found a church family! Phil, a devoted follower of Jesus, played in the worship band and became an instant friend to every person he met. What blessed me most was when Phil would say, "I learned grace for the first time here at God's Club."

One middle-aged couple, Ted and Susie, added wisdom and spirituality. They had both grown up in rigidly conservative churches, but had recently been discovering the freedom of true grace and wanted to be part of our mission to bring that message to a younger demographic. Their authenticity and love drew many people to them as they exercised leadership in the church.

We had a lady come to worship whose husband had cheated on her. They are now divorced. The Gold Club is where he met his affair person.

Someone brought a friend, who was an architect. I remember thinking, "Now that's what we need—a high earner, and he will bring his professional friends." He was one big mess. He had been a cocaine addict for twenty years and was three weeks sober. Everyone was welcome!

On that first Sunday, someone dropped a check in the offering plate for $5,000. A few weeks later, I was able to speak to the donors, Ricky and Sharon, and hear their story. "We have not been involved in church in a while, but we love the Lord. As soon as we walked in here, we both knew this was home." They went on to explain, "We recently sold our business, but have been slack about our giving. We wanted to do a catch-up offering."

One of the many creatives who joined our journey was Edward. Shy, with blonde hair that was always mussed up, Edward played bass guitar in the praise band. Our worship minister had worked with this young man in another context and had invited him to help with the praise band. Edward had quite a background. When he was just 15 years old, Edward's father took his own life. This began a long, dark journey into opioids and other drugs, which eventually led to heroin. He was in and out of treatment.

"Getting involved in Christian Church Buckhead was one of the best things that ever happened to me," Edward told me recently. "I had a community of people who were seeking my good, and the preaching kept me in touch with God. Being at church always reminded me there was a god who didn't want me high."

As he grew in the Lord and in his involvement with the church, Edward and his family made important decisions about getting help. I'm happy to report he is now clean and sober.

If there was one highlight that stood out on Kick-off Sunday, in a day filled with special moments, it was the joy of seeing the front row of worship seats occupied by former dancers, some of whom had worked in this very room when it was the Gold Club.

One lady who was there, Micki, said she danced at the Gold Club years ago when it was Atlanta's top venue. Her stage name was "Tisha" and she remembers performing in a place she recalls as "dirty" during a time that was "just a blur." Now a nurse living in a suburb of Atlanta, Micki's own transformation could be seen as she sang her heart out during songs of praise. "I got a sense of peace and chills, a cleansing feeling."

Others commented on the "feeling" in the room, the atmosphere.

Lauren sensed the power of the Holy Spirit. "It was tangible in God's Club."

Derrick reflected that "you could have a terrible day and walk into God's Club and it all disappeared."

Marla and many others said it felt like "family."

Not only were those who attended and involved in the church affected by the teaching, friendships, and the larger story of transformation at play, their preacher/leader was impacted in a big way, too. This project was by far the biggest leadership challenge of my life. The enormity of the task, as well as dealing with so many unknown factors and the unpredictability related to renovating an old building in such a short time, tested my resilience, faith, patience, and energy.

At home, my son and daughter were adjusting to moving from a small town where their dad was a pastor and almost everyone knew everyone. They left friends, a thriving children's ministry, trips to their friend's farm, and the familiarity of the one place they had known as home for their entire lives.

Most pastors, when they move to a new church setting, do not find themselves needing to explain "strip club" to their seven and nine-year olds. My daughter had sort of pieced together a fair idea of what was going on, based on hearing the adults talk about plans and goals around our dinner table. But my son was another story. I sat on the bed with him and tried to explain that sometimes men pay to see women take their clothes off. He just thought that was "gross." Trying to protect his innocence while also including him and his sister as part of the renovation was probably my biggest hurdle. But they did great, and hopefully weren't traumatized for the rest of their lives!

On top of dealing with two young children trying to get situated, Carol was also dealing with setting up a new house, creating a classroom in the basement for home-schooling, and leaving a support system of church, friends, and neighbors. It was fairly stressful at our house.

Sometimes I would go on the roof of God's Club, just to look out over the city and think. One afternoon I was joined by Mark, who came to us from a large African-American church, after reading one of the newspaper articles. He said he came to CCB because he felt led. We stood silently by the ledge for a few moments, and then I shared about being discouraged—the heat in the building kept breaking down, problems with the electrical, and the ever-present finances. Mark turned, placed his hand on my shoulder, and encouraged me, "Dan, God called you to this. He will do it. You're the man to lead." That truly made a difference in my spirit and attitude.

Lesson one: God specializes in restoration and resurrection. He can redeem you, too. If you allow him to clean out some of your old "stuff" and give him room to work, he will restore, refurbish, renovate, rebuild, re-create, and rejuvenate.

Lesson two: even though I could not "see" them ahead of time, God was bringing the people to join our church family.

Conclusion

There is a common thread running through the reflections and memories of those of us who were part of this bold undertaking. I heard repeated multiple times, "This is what the church is all about."

I have sat with this sentiment, analyzing and appreciating its weight. I believe what so many of us gained from the God's Club journey was seeing the love of Christ being exercised in a very practical way. Most followers of Jesus long for opportunities to truly put their faith into action and to enjoy the satisfaction which comes from using their gifts to bless others. What seemed to be exhilarating about planting this new spiritual outpost was the privilege of living out the purpose of the church, God's earthly family, which is meant to assume a posture of service, humility, and of course, love.

The transitioning of the Gold Club into a church was a simple and visible metaphor of how the heavenly Father works in our lives. We could see it. We understood the complexity as well as the simplicity of that image.

God changes buildings and people from being broken to restored.

From ugly to beautiful.

From meaningless to useful.

It was happening right before our eyes and reminded us that each of us can experience that same power of new beginnings. Over 200 volunteers from our church and churches around metro Atlanta came and helped with the renovation. They wanted to be part of creating a new thing.

See, I am doing a new thing!
Now it springs up; do you not perceive it?
I am making a way in the wilderness
and streams in the wasteland.

Isaiah 43:19

The reimagined facility became a beautiful tapestry of who we were and what we were doing here. That old, empty building, which formerly operated as a den of sin, became the space where sinners were welcome, and crushed spirits were restored.

The promise of 2 Corinthians 5:17 was spoken and received frequently within those walls, "Therefore, if anyone is in Christ, the new creation has come: the old has gone. The new is here!"

It made me smile to think about the words of restoration that were spoken, sung, and recited in a room filled with mirrors, which once reflected decadence, now reflecting the faces of the forgiven!

We thought we were going to start a church for urban professionals, meeting in a tasteful setting. We did create ministry with that target group, plus multiple others, just in a very different context. This isn't what we planned, but it's where the Spirit took us.

Dan M. Garrett

Many are the plans in a person's heart,
but it is the Lord's purpose that prevails.

Proverbs 19:21

From the beginning, the trajectory for the church was set by our values.

- ❖ We will preach Jesus and not ourselves.

- ❖ We will truly welcome every person.

- ❖ We will teach and practice grace.

- ❖ We will seek diversity.

- ❖ We will have fun.

By God's grace, we lived out all those values.

I'm not sure what anyone will say at my funeral, but if all that's said is, "He loved people on the margins his whole life, and one of those places was on Piedmont Road where he started a church in an old club," I'll be fine with that.

Addendum

How did you get so much press?

The church renovation was featured on the cover of the Atlanta paper at least twice, and received additional exposure through radio and television interviews, and lots of word of mouth.

Probably, the most significant factor was the article being sent out by the Associated Press all over the world.

We didn't pay for any marketing for the first 3 months.

What happened to the dancers?

As for the ladies who once worked at the Gold Club, many left that world through a terrific ministry, Victoria's Friends, which counsels, offers financial assistance, and directs the women toward healthy and productive lives.

A lady in our church volunteered with this ministry. They actually go into the club dressing rooms (with the blessing of the managers) and take baskets to the ladies who work there. They pray with them and leave them a card with a number if they want to talk further. Many come out of the lifestyle through this ministry.

A dozen of the ladies, some of whom had danced in the Gold Club, came to the opening of Christian Church Buckhead. They proudly gathered and sat in the front row. It's incredible to try to imagine their emotions of praying and singing praises to God in the exact same space where they once performed, while probably high. This is the transforming power of Almighty God. One of the former dancers said it was "cleansing" to be there for our opening day. Wow!

A few weeks after our opening day, Victoria's Friends held one of their monthly meetings in the very building where their members once felt trapped.

Is the church still meeting there?

No. As special as the building was, and even though we had become strangely attached, it became necessary for us to move to another location. There was just too much cost associated with renting and maintaining a building of that age. Once we moved, the building sat empty for a few years and has recently been turned into a special event venue.

What about Christian Church Buckhead today?

Our growing group left God's Club and began meeting at the AMC Theatres at the elegant Phipps Plaza a few blocks away. Every Sunday morning, a team of volunteers would meet the U-Haul truck at the mall loading ramp area at six-thirty and unload sound equipment, video projectors, tables, chairs, and tons of other stuff needed to make "church" happen. While some of us set up one theater for kids and another one for worship, the band would practice, and the food team would get the concession stand ready with donuts and coffee. And after worship, we would haul it all back down the freight elevator to the truck.

After two years at the theatres, we moved into a "real" building on Peachtree Street. A church group had moved in anticipation of Hilton erecting a mammoth complex on that corner. But the recession hit, and Hilton abandoned their plans.

In our frail, human, doubting minds, we could never have pictured being right on the main street of Atlanta in a beautiful, modern building. The church, only a few years after starting, was in the most visible section of Buckhead.

I resigned at the end of 2006 and passed the baton to a trusted friend and former member of my Mt. Carmel youth group, Derek Sweatman. As pastor and a gifted teacher/leader, he brought a powerful energy and vision to reach the city.

Derek likes to tell this story on himself. He visited God's Club during the messy renovation and literally said, "I would never work here."

I remind him of this comment occasionally, just to point out God has a fun sense of humor.

After five years in the Peachtree Road facility, Christian Church Buckhead moved from Buckhead to downtown and needed to change the name. They became Atlanta Christian Church, purchased and renovated a church building, and settled into their new home where they continue to minister today.

The narrative of lives being changed continues. And the heart of the church remains the same ... to reach hurting people from every background, with a simple message of grace and redemption.

Gratitude

As we celebrate the twentieth anniversary of the birth of Christian Church Buckhead, it's impossible to list all the names of those who contributed to the success of this enterprise.

However, I do want to acknowledge the dedication and sacrifice of some individuals who played key roles in the early days.

Ministry staff: Lindsey Feus, Karen Kabakoff, Chris Smith, Rae Tyler, Jamie Vernon, and Mark Wall.

The production of *From Poles to Pews*, my first book, would not have happened without meaningful and wise input from a variety of friends, including LeRoy Lawson, Mark Taylor, Alan Scott, Jennifer Taylor Johnson, Ryan McCarty, Lane Byrum, Ward Jenkins, Jim Barber, Aaron Chambers, and Shawn McMullen. Special thanks goes to the wonderful editor, Elizabeth Maynard Charle.

I'm especially grateful for my family. This photo is from the year we launched the church, 2004. Campbell, Carol, Danielle, and Dan (and Maggie the dog)

Dan M. Garrett

About the Author

Dan Garrett is an ordained minister and graduate of Cincinnati Christian University.

At 24 years old, he began as youth minister at a large church in Decatur, Georgia and served there 11 years. During that time, Dan helped start Arrive Alive, a nationwide school assembly program equipping students to make positive choices. He also founded and led Home Team Conferences, bringing teens and parents together around the nation. For many years, Dan volunteered with Camp Sunshine for children with cancer.

In addition to speaking, teaching, and training through conferences and seminars, Dan has pastored a small-town church, planted a church in Buckhead in Atlanta and led a suburban church in Roswell, Georgia.

He now serves pastors and churches through Christian City, a ministry of housing, health, and hope, with 1000 children and adults living on 500 acres just below the Atlanta airport.

Dan has spoken to over two million people in 35 states and internationally. His greatest joy is being husband to Carol and father to their adult children, Danielle and Campbell.

https://dangarrett.org/

Made in the USA
Columbia, SC
19 February 2024

31807232R00067